WITHDRAWN

LIFE AFTER BIRTH

LIFE
AFTER
BIRTH

Practical Exercises for Spiritual Growth

BILL McKEE

TYNDALE HOUSE PUBLISHERS
Wheaton, Illinois

COVERDALE HOUSE PUBLISHERS LTD.
London, England

46442

Other books by Bill McKee:
Happy Hang Up
Shut Your Generation Gap
Orbit of Ashes

Bible quotations are from *The Living Bible, Paraphrased,* except where otherwise indicated, and are used by permission of Tyndale House Publishers.

Library of Congress Catalog Card Number 72-97659
ISBN 8423-2190-X

Copyright © 1973 Tyndale House Publishers, Wheaton, Illinois

First printing, June 1973

Printed in the United States of America

CONTENTS

CONGRATULATIONS, CHRISTIAN!

You're a royal child now, a brand new person in the family of God!

Really? Right! God says in John 1:12 that when you receive Jesus Christ as Savior you are a child of God. That's some kind of royalty! "But now the Lord who created you, O Israel, says, Don't be afraid, for I have ransomed you; I have called you by name; you are mine" (Isaiah 43:1).

When you prayed and asked Christ to come into your life, he heard your prayer, for, "Whosoever shall call upon the name of the Lord shall be saved." There is a difference between believing and receiving: some believe but the belief stays in the mind and produces only decent churchgoers. That's sad because such people have taken a preliminary step. You're different, though, if you have received Jesus Christ. This genuine, transforming faith also comes from God, as Paul tells us in Ephesians 2:8: "Because of his kindness you have been saved through trusting Christ. And even trusting is not of yourselves; it too is a gift from God."

In a supernatural way, you became a child of God through being *born again*. Jesus assured us this is super-important. "With all the earnestness I possess I tell you this: unless you are born again, you can never get into the kingdom of God" (John 3:3).

Do you remember when you were born physically—like, what color was the doctor's eyes? Were his hands cold? Did he slap hard? You can't quite recall? The easiest thing that ever happened to you was being born — but it cost your mother plenty!

Being born into God's family is also easy — for you. A simple but honest prayer of faith in Jesus is enough. But this second birth cost God a great deal — the death on a cross of his only begotten Son. The penalty for sin is death, and Jesus took that penalty to spare you. Now you are free to live with him forever! (Romans 3:23; 6:23)

Just remember — spiritually you are very young. You need nourishment, encouragement, exercise, and training. Nobody becomes an adult overnight, but they don't quit the human race on that account. Now you must give God a chance to prove what a difference he can make in your life. As you walk with him, you'll be amazed how fast you can grow. And you'll begin to understand things that are foggy and uncertain now.

On the following pages you'll find nourishment, encouragement, and exercise for your newborn spirit. You'll also find a few warnings and some effective antidotes for infection and spills. The growing Christian life is exciting. And, like the psalmist David, "The joy of the Lord is your strength!" Your Father wants you to be happy; wants you to be strong; wants you to be successful in the highest sense — and you can be by growing into the image of God's Son, your Savior (Romans 8:29).

So here we go on a one-month adventure with God. Expect the best — of yourself and God. "Long to grow up into the fullness of your salvation: cry for this as a baby cries for his milk" (1 Peter 2:3).

YOU'RE SPECIAL TO GOD

"For you have been chosen by God himself — you are priests of the King, you are holy and pure, you are God's very own. . . . Once you were less than nothing; now you are God's own. Once you knew very little of God's kindness; now your very lives have been changed by it. Dear brothers, you are only visitors here. Since your real home is in heaven I beg you to keep away from the evil pleasures of this world; they are not for you, for they fight against your very souls" (1 Peter 2: 9-11).

Jesus said God knows even the number of hairs in our heads; no one else ever loved me enough to check that out! We must be very special to God. "I am the Good Shepherd and know my own sheep," said Jesus, "and they know me. . . . I lay down my life for the sheep" (John 10:14, 15). We will never get beyond the care of this Shepherd.

God keeps records. That could shake you up — if you didn't realize what he has done with your evil deeds and "secret" sins.

"He has not punished us as we deserve for all our sins, for his mercy toward those who fear and honor him is as great as the height of the heavens above the

11

earth. He has removed our sins as far away from us as the east is from the west. He is like a father to us, tender and sympathetic to those who reverence him. He is merciful and tender toward those who don't deserve it; he is slow to get angry and full of kindness and love. He never bears a grudge" (Psalm 103:10-13, 8, 9).

That's your heavenly Father — and your new heritage. God loves you so much you can't handle it — as Psalm 23 puts it: your "cup runs over." That sure beats the old emptiness and thirst, doesn't it?

What to do today:

Every time you take a drink — of water, pop, coffee, tea, or milk — tell Jesus: "Thank you for loving me and filling my heart."

2

THE THREE PARTS OF THEE

You were created in three dimensions: body, soul (or mind), and spirit. We come into the world most conscious of the physical dimension, demanding food, comfort, sleep, caresses. And we're very vocal if these bodily senses are not satisfied.

Some of us get hung up in the physical dimension. We use our other dimensions to pamper this one. Money, pleasure, and material things are the big bags. Our happiness is measured by satisfaction in our physical dimension.

We're not very old when we discover the role of intelligence. School develops this dimension, and when we learn to read and calculate, the sky's the limit to our capacity for learning. We can assimilate phenomenal amounts of knowledge, yet our very educated society is in serious trouble today. We have theories and programs but few workable answers to crime, drugs, divorce, moral decay, alcoholism, racism, war, poverty, and pollution.

So a wise man looks further for help. And he rediscovers the spiritual dimension. Of course, it's been there all the time, but after a childish encounter with Sunday school, commercialized Christmases and Easters, and stained-glass fantasies, most people reject it as anti-intellectual or nice-but-later, thanks.

13

Human beings who try to make it on two dimensions are frustrated folks. There's no way to get it all together, and that drives some of them nuts. It's a kind of blindness, said the Apostle Paul: "The spiritual man has insight into everything, and that bothers and baffles the man of the world who can't understand him at all" (1 Corinthians 2:15).

But now that you have received Christ, the spiritual dimension is alive! It's up to you to put your priorities straight and keep your spiritual dimension first in your life. Listen to what the Bible says about this: "**And no one can ever lay any other real foundation than that one we already have — Jesus Christ**" (1 Corinthians 3:11).

Now the spiritual can immensely influence your thinking and your emotions as well as the use of your marvelous body. God has made you a whole *person!* Every dimension can be more beautiful as our Creator intended. His first creations were perfect — and your spiritual re-creation has started you on the way to ultimate perfection in Christ.

Notice what Jesus said in Matthew 22:37. "Love the Lord your God with all your heart, soul, and mind. This is the first and greatest commandment." In learning to obey this commandment, you will find your body and spirit increasingly sensitized to God along with your conscious thoughts.

What to do today:

Remind yourself to keep your priorities straight. If you're home, set an alarm or a timer a couple of times to jog you. If at school or work, pause at recess or lunch to check whether your body, emotions, or God-sensitive spirit is motivating you. And ask your heavenly Father to help you.

3

DOUBT

Yesterday's exercise in priorities may have caused you to realize that changing your ideas is not easy. You've got to work at it until your mind runs in new grooves. If you found yourself going through a whole day without thinking about spiritual matters, you're a set-up for a bad infection of doubt. You may even be wondering if your prayer of repentance was heard.

Did God really do those things like forgiving my sins and accepting me as his very own? I felt so good then, but now I feel more down than ever.

There are two words in that last sentence that expose your disease: "felt" and "feel." Feelings are like a roller coaster — you're flying high and feeling fine one moment and then you hit a downer . . . zoom! The joyride is over; welcome back to the human race!

But remember, your new life is not based on feelings; it's based on *Christ*. And Christ hasn't changed. "Jesus Christ is the same yesterday, today, and forever!" (Hebrews 13:8).

Everyone has been disappointed by people. Some made promises they didn't keep and others changed their minds and left us hanging. Your heavenly Father will never do that. You've found someone you can trust completely, forever. So don't measure God by changing circumstances — he's not affected!

"Now we can look forward to the salvation God has promised us. There is no longer any room for doubt. And we can tell others that salvation is ours, for there is no question that he will do what he says. In response to all he has done for us, let us outdo each other in being helpful and kind to each other and in doing good" (Hebrews 10:23, 24).

What to do today:

Tell God how you feel and praise him that he is as strong and loving and faithful as the day you invited him into your life as Savior and Lord.

And for your encouragement: "Remember your leaders who have taught you the Word of God. Think of all the good that has come from their lives, and try to trust the Lord as they do" (Hebrews 13:7).

4

HEY! I GOT JOY

You've been happy, you've known pleasure, you've cracked up at a joke, you've been thrilled and excited. Well, now you've got *joy! Real* joy!

Humans can't manufacture joy — any more than we can get wisdom. We can produce pleasure and knowledge, but true joy and wisdom are exclusive gifts from God to his children. ". . . beauty for ashes; joy instead of mourning; praise instead of heaviness. Instead of shame and dishonor, you shall have a double portion of prosperity and everlasting joy" (Isaiah 61:3, 7).

Joy is like an ocean. During a storm the winds lash waves into boiling turmoil, but down in the depths there is perfect calm. We all pop off now and then or we overreact. We worry and get upset. Sometimes problems push us around pretty bad. Before Christ, our lives were so shallow that situations like that would leave us roiled and full of despair. But now we have a deep reserve of joy to draw from. When we consider that we were spiritually lost but now are saved, our other problems shrink to their proper proportions in life; though our problems may be serious, we have much to be thankful and to praise God for.

"To enjoy your work and to accept your lot in life — that is indeed a gift from God. The person who does that will not need to look back with sorrow on his past, for God gives him joy" (Ecclesiastes 5:20).

God knows you very well. Remember, he personally designed and made you, and he wants you to be joyful. That doesn't mean you're to walk around with a phony smile that makes people want an aspirin. Nor does it call for a condescending attitude toward "less fortunate" beings. It's just a supernatural power that you know is within. Man, just knowing it's there excites me.

I remember a news article about the Jesus People that said their smiles bugged people. Like they had some "inner joke" others didn't know about. Right on! That is joy! Jesus tells us how to keep it deep and running over.

"Live within my love. When you obey me you are living in my love, just as I obey my Father and live in his love. I have told you this so that you will be filled with my joy. Yes, your cup of joy will overflow" (John 15: 9-11).

So if you feel weak and doubts creep in, or God seems to have forgotten you, come on back to the well of joy and get strong by renewing your obedience to the God of your salvation.

What to do today:

First, tell God thanks for supplying the deep joy you don't even know how to use yet. Thank him again for your salvation.

Don't gripe today! Keep it positive. Notice how different life is when you practice the joy of the Lord.

5

"MIRROR, MIRROR ON THE WALL"

This little exercise can put spiritual muscle in your soul. You've had a few vitamins to increase your energy; now it's time for some deep-down strength.

Take one of the printed verses out of the book and tape it to your bathroom mirror. Beginning now and whenever you're in front of the mirror, filter that verse through your mind. You've brushed your teeth, washed your hands, and combed your hair enough to do them without thinking, so really concentrate on the Bible verse. Try to memorize it. Remember every time you are at the mirror to give your mind to that verse.

At first it may seem a waste of time because your mind isn't conditioned to memorize the Bible. But before long you'll begin to experience that wisdom we've talked about. And God will help you memorize his Word if you really want to obey him in this command.

"You must think constantly about these commandments" (Deuteronomy 6:6). "How can a young man stay pure? By reading your Word and following its rules. I have tried my best to find you — don't let me wander off from your instructions. I have thought much about your words, and stored them in my heart so that they would hold me back from sin" (Psalm 119:9-11).

Those words were written by a person just like you — not perfect but determined not to chicken out, either.

Obviously, this discipline helped him since he was later referred to by God as "a man after my own heart." So take this proven exercise and make it a joyful discipline in your life.

Then just before you go to sleep, try to say the verse by memory. If you can, put up a new one in the morning. I guarantee you will experience amazing changes in your life by doing this for thirty days.

You'll notice the memory verses are in both the King James and *The Living Bible* versions, so you can use whichever one is better for you.

What to do today:

Cut out a verse, tape it to the bathroom mirror, and follow through as you've read.

P.S. If you hang in there, you'll see faster achievements with this than through any other spiritual exercise I know.

For God loved the world so much that he gave his only Son so that anyone who believes in him shall not perish but have eternal life.
(John 3:16, TLB)

Because of his kindness you have been saved through trusting Christ. And even trusting is not of yourselves; it too is a gift from God.

Salvation is not a reward for the good we have done, so none of us can take any credit for it.
(Ephesians 2:8, 9, TLB)

Don't be anxious about tomorrow. God will take care of your tomorrow too. Live one day at a time.
(Matthew 6:34, TLB)

You haven't tried this before. Ask, using my name, and you will receive, and your cup of joy will overflow.
(John 16:24, TLB)

We know these things are true by believing, not by seeing.
(2 Corinthians 5:7, TLB)

Look! I have been standing at the door and I am constantly knocking. If anyone hears me calling him and opens the door, I will come in and fellowship with him and he with me.
(Revelation 3:20, TLB)

The Holy Spirit, God's Gift, does not want you to be afraid of people, but to be wise and strong, and to love them and enjoy being with them.
(2 Timothy 1:7, TLB)

Be delighted with the Lord. Then he will give you all your heart's desires.
(Psalm 37:4, TLB)

For by grace are ye saved through faith; and that not of yourselves: it is the gift of God: Not of works, lest any man should boast.

(Ephesians 2:8, 9)

For God so loved the world, that he gave his only begotten Son, that whosoever believeth in him should not perish, but have everlasting life.

(John 3:16)

Hitherto have ye asked nothing in my name: ask, and ye shall receive, that your joy may be full.

(John 16:24)

Take therefore no thought for the morrow: for the morrow shall take thought for the things of itself. Sufficient unto the day is the evil thereof.

(Matthew 6:34)

Behold, I stand at the door, and knock: if any man hear my voice, and open the door, I will come in to him, and will sup with him, and he with me.

(Revelation 3:20)

For we walk by faith, not by sight.

(2 Corinthians 5:7)

Delight thyself also in the Lord; and he shall give thee the desires of thine heart.

(Psalm 37:4)

For God hath not given us the spirit of fear; but of power, and of love, and of a sound mind.

(2 Timothy 1:7)

How can a young man stay pure? By reading your Word and following its rules. I have tried my best to find you — don't let me wander off from your instructions. I have thought much about your words, and stored them in my heart so that they would hold me back from sin.

(Psalm 119:9-11, TLB)

And what is it that God has said? That he has given us eternal life, and that this life is in his Son. So whoever has God's Son has life; whoever does not have his Son, does not have life. I have written this to you who believe in the Son of God so that you may know you have eternal life.

(1 John 5:11-13, TLB)

The spiritual man has insight into everything, and that bothers and baffles the man of the world, who can't understand him at all.

(1 Corinthians 2:15, TLB)

If we confess our sins to him, he can be depended on to forgive us and to cleanse us from every wrong. And it is perfectly proper for God to do this for us because Christ died to wash away our sins.

(1 John 1:9, TLB)

To all who received him, he gave the right to become children of God. All they needed to do was to trust him to save them.

(John 1:12, TLB)

Happy is the man who doesn't give in and do wrong when he is tempted, for afterwards he will get as his reward the crown of life that God has promised those who love him.

(James 1:12, TLB)

25

And this is the record, that God hath given to us eternal life, and this life is in his Son. He that hath the Son hath life; and he that hath not the Son of God hath not life. These things have I written unto you that believe on the name of the Son of God; that ye may know that ye have eternal life, and that ye may believe on the name of the Son of God.

(1 John 5:11-13)

If we confess our sins, he is faithful and just to forgive us our sins, and to cleanse us from all unrighteousness.

(1 John 1:9)

Blessed is the man that endureth temptation: for when he is tried, he shall receive the crown of life, which the Lord hath promised to them that love him.

(James 1:12)

Wherewithal shall a young man cleanse his way? By taking heed thereto according to thy word. With my whole heart have I sought thee: O let me not wander from thy commandments. Thy word have I hid in mine heart, that I might not sin against thee.

(Psalm 119:9-11)

But he that is spiritual judgeth all things, yet he himself is judged of no man.

(1 Corinthians 2:15)

But as many as received him, to them gave he power to become the sons of God, even to them that believe on his name. (John 1:12)

PRACTICE HIS PRESENCE

Most of us eat a few times a day, so meals are a good reminder for you to remember what you might have forgotten . . . while you're rereading that to make sense of it, I'll get on to a project that explains it and at the same time coordinates very well with the verse in the mirror.

When you pause to pray before eating breakfast, tell the Lord you're going to "practice his presence" between breakfast and lunch. This means you're not going to even think about the afternoon but really try to sense his nearness during the morning.

I think you know I don't mean you should be so heavenly minded that you are no earthly good. For example, don't neglect talking to somebody because you're practicing Jesus' presence. Or don't feel compelled to take a day off work! Learn to acknowledge Jesus with you wherever you are. When you realize he's there, you're going to feel more strength and calmness.

At coffee break or lunch take a few seconds to say thanks for the morning's companionship, then tell him you're going to practice his presence that afternoon. You'll find this private experience real fun — there you are in a strife-wracked world enjoying fellowship with the Prince of Peace!

Next is dinner (or "supper"). You might have to admit you blew it and forgot all about him. Go ahead!

Don't try to con God; you'll lose everytime. Tell him you are going to "practice his presence" between dinner and bedtime.

You may go out, work, read, etc., but if you include him by keeping him close to the surface of your thinking you'll find everything going better.

Jesus said, "So don't be anxious about tomorrow. God will take care of your tomorrow too. Live one day at a time!" (Matthew 6:34).

What to do today:

Tie this exercise in with the mirror thing; start with the verse, then use the natural pauses of the day (breakfast, coffee breaks, lunch, and dinner) as reminders to practice his presence.

7

OOPS!

You blew it! Right? And you feel miserable because you thought you wouldn't foul up like you did before you became a Christian.

Well, as long as you're in that suit of bones and skin, you're going to stumble and fall. The key to how often you stumble and how hard you fall is how fast you pick yourself up, and ask God's forgiveness, and start moving again.

Remember you're still a child spiritually, and walking spiritually results in soul bruises and falls. I've never heard of a baby learning to walk without falling. The beautiful sight to parents, though, is when the child pushes up and tries again. What a heartbreak if the child should lie sobbing and never learn to walk and run and jump!

Your heavenly Father knows you will stumble, and he's made arrangements for your joy to be restored through forgiveness. "But if we confess our sins to him, he can be depended on to forgive us and to cleanse us from every wrong" (1 John 1:9).

Whatever you do, don't try to cover up or excuse your sin. That's like putting a Band-aid over a sliver in your finger. It's going to hurt a lot more later. "Don't be misled," said Paul. "Remember that you can't ignore God and get away with it; a man will always reap just the kind of crop he sows. If he sows to please his own wrong desires he will be planting seeds of evil and he will surely reap a harvest of spiritual decay and death; but if he plants the good things of the Spirit, he will reap the everlasting life which the Holy Spirit gives him. And let us not get tired of doing what is right, for after a while we will reap a harvest of blessing if we don't get discouraged and give up. That's why whenever we can we should always be kind to everyone, and especially to our Christian brothers" (Galatians 6:7-10).

What to do today:

Tell God honestly when you have sinned and ask him to forgive you. Never mind how often you have to ask — when you stop asking is when infection sets in; keep getting up and taking another step.

DON'T LISTEN

An underlying cause for "Oops! Goofed again" is a voice that makes sin sound harmless and reasonable. Since this voice is with us, we had better be able to identify it and turn off our receiver. That inner voice is the influence of Satan. He is your enemy, and he accuses you of your weakness and past failures.

He is a master of disguises and can even fake it as an "angel of light" (2 Corinthians 11:14). He is often represented by a brilliant professor who denies God and gently mocks your faith as "nonintellectual." Or as a slick swinger who tells you how gratifying the "new morality" is. He may whisper his encouragement about problems in your life. "Go ahead and make others miserable; they don't understand how you suffer." Or, "You deserve that drink; you work hard. Indulge yourself!" Or, "Don't be weird! Everybody else is doing it." Or, "If you cheat just a little it's OK. · If you don't, somebody else will." Or, "Demand your way! Let the chips fall where they will — that's life."

Those are just a few of Satan's favorites, but he knows where you're weak and that's where he will attack. He is raging at you for accepting Christ, but remember this:

"Dear young friends, you belong to God and have already won your fight with those who are against Christ, because there is someone in your hearts who is stronger than any evil teacher in this wicked world" (1 John 4:4).

So you see, the Christ you received has already defeated Satan — and you need to keep on claiming that victory by faith.

"No one who has become a part of God's family makes a practice of sinning, for Christ, God's Son, holds him securely and the devil cannot get his hands on him. We know that we are children of God and that all the rest of the world around us is under Satan's power and control. And we know that Christ, God's Son, has come to help us understand and find the true God. And now we are in God because we are in Jesus Christ, his Son, who is the only true God; and he is eternal Life. Dear children, keep away from everything that might take God's place in your hearts" (1 John 5:18-21).

What to do today:

When the voice of temptation speaks, either within you or through someone else, recognize the evil source and turn to God quickly. Ask God for strength, then do something to occupy your body and mind wholesomely — don't just stand there and get wiped out.

Satan used you and pushed you around; now he can't "get his hand" on you — he can only talk. Tune him out and tune in Christ.

SUPER-POWER

The moment you received Christ, God gave you an arm-load of the most wonderful gifts anyone could ever receive.

He forgave your sin and removed the guilt from your life. "So there is now no condemnation awaiting those who belong to Christ Jesus. For the power of the life-giving Spirit — and this power is mine through Christ Jesus — has freed me from the vicious circle of sin and death" (Romans 8:1, 2).

He assured you of eternal life. "And what is it that God has said? That he has given us eternal life, and that this life is in his Son. So whoever has God's Son has life; whoever does not have his Son does not have life. I have written this to you who believe in the Son of God so that you may know you have eternal life" (1 John 5:11-13).

Without this next gift we could not know joy or peace or victory in our lives *now!* God gave us the Person of the Holy Spirit to dwell in us and help us. "No one can know God's thoughts except God's own Spirit. And God has actually given us his Spirit (not the world's spirit) to tell us about the wonderful free gifts of grace and blessing that God has given us" (1 Corinthians 2:11, 12).

This is the voice to listen to and obey! He knows that we are born with a natural inclination to do wrong, and since an evil voice from the outside tempts our natural attraction to evil we need all the help we can get. And *we have* all the help we need — if we call on the Holy Spirit.

"I advise you to obey only the Holy Spirit's instructions. He will tell you where to go and what to do. And then you won't always be doing the wrong things your evil nature wants you to. For we naturally love to do evil things that are just the opposite from the things that the Holy Spirit tells us to do; and the good things we want to do when the Holy Spirit has his way with us are just the opposite of our natural desires. These two forces within us are constantly fighting each other to win control over us" (Galatians 5:16, 17).

You are the controlling factor, though, of both forces. If you get in the habit of listening to the wrong voice, the Holy Spirit will be quenched and your life will slide back toward the old rut. But if you keep reading that verse in the mirror, think about the depth of joy, ask forgiveness fast, and get going again for God you'll remain sensitive to this great, pure power in you. Before long, you'll be anticipating the right instead of being alert to the wrong.

Check the following comparison chart based on Galatians 5:19-23, 25.

NATURAL	SPIRITUAL
"But when you follow your own wrong inclinations your lives will produce these evil results:	"But when the Holy Spirit controls our lives he will produce this kind of fruit in us:

impure thoughts	love
eagerness for lustful pleasure	joy
idolatry (materialism)	peace
spiritism (astrology, witchcraft, etc.)	patience
hatred and fighting	kindness
jealousy and anger	goodness
constant effort to get the best for yourself	faithfulness
complaints and criticisms	gentleness
the feeling that everyone else is wrong except those in your own little group	self-control

and there will be wrong
  doctrine
  envy
  murder
  drunkenness
  wild parties and all that
  sort of thing.

"Let me tell you again anyone living that sort of life will not inherit the kingdom of God."

"If we are living now by the Holy Spirit's power, let us follow the Holy Spirit's leading in every part of our lives."

What to do today:

Really concentrate to sense the Holy Spirit's leading. Remember, he isn't in you to take away your fun or make you miserable. (Don't listen to that lie of Satan.) He lives in you to bring victory and joy and peace.

You're going to obey him many times today and see evidences of the "spiritual" column in your thoughts, words, and conduct. When you do, pause and say thanks.

Whew! This is exciting! Who could imagine that good, *super*-natural things like this would happen to *me*. (The following are expressions to use after the sentence above — whichever you prefer.)

Wow!
Far out!
Wonderful!
So fine!
Ummmmmm!
Dig it!
Outta sight!
Praise the Lord!

Selah!
Too much!
Glory!
Thank you, Jesus!
Praise-a-luia!
Halleglory!
Mugus!
Really!

YOUR CHURCH

Find a good church. By a good church, I don't mean one with just beauty and friendly people. I mean one that preaches the Bible as God's absolutely reliable revelation and Jesus Christ as the eternal Son of God and our Savior from sin. If they're reluctant to talk about humanity's need for repentance and forgiveness, they don't know your Savior. Pass!

One way to find a Bible-preaching church is to go with the person who led you to Christ. Or if you came to Christ in a church, that one should be a good place to learn more about your Lord.

Don't get caught in the web of traditionalism: "Our family has always gone to this church so I suppose I should too." But tradition doesn't save you, nor does it produce spiritual growth. God's Word is your spiritual milk and meat.

It is dangerous to lack association with a good church. "Let us not neglect our church meetings, as some people do, but encourage and warn each other, especially now that the day of his coming back is drawing near" (Hebrews 10:25).

Many people criticize churches as being filled with hypocrites and having nothing relevant to our times. That is very true of some churches, but lots of churches are really with it. Both you and the church are weaker when you don't get together.

Jesus calls the true Church his "body" — of which he is the head. He is referring to true believers who have trusted him as Savior, not to a building or religious group that has taken the name "church." He wants believers to fellowship and work with other members of his spiritual body in service and growth. "Our bodies have many parts, but the many parts make up only one body when they are all put together. So it is with the 'body' of Christ" (1 Corinthians 12:12).

Worshiping, learning, and serving together brings definite changes. "We will no longer be like children, forever changing our minds about what we believe because someone has told something different, or has cleverly lied to us and made the lie sound like the truth. Instead, we will lovingly follow the truth at all times — speaking truly, dealing truly, living truly — and so become more and more in every way like Christ who is the head of his body, the Church. Under his direction the whole body is fitted together perfectly, and each part in its own special way helps the other parts, so that the whole body is healthy and growing and full of love" (Ephesians 4:14-16)

What to do today:

Check with the one who led you to Christ about his church. Go to church with a desire to learn. Try to overlook people's weaknesses and failings and look for the positive and good. After getting your bruises in the world for a week, use Sunday for spiritual renewal in the fellowship of others who love your Lord.

11

GOOD-ALL-AROUND FATHER

This is going to be a good day, so let loose with one of those words of praise again! You've got a truly great Father in heaven — he really is looking out for you.

He guides you. "Trust the Lord completely . . . in everything you do, put God first, and he will direct you and crown your efforts with success" (Proverbs 3:5, 6).

He's behind you. "And if you leave God's paths and go astray, you will hear a Voice behind you say, 'No, this is the way; walk here" (Isaiah 30:21).

He's under you. "The eternal God is your refuge, and underneath are the everlasting arms" (Deuteronomy 33: 27).

He's above you. "He descends from the heavens in majestic splendor to help you" (Deuteronomy 33:26).

He's on one side. "There are 'friends' who pretend to be friends, but there is a friend who sticks closer than a brother" (Proverbs 18:24).

He's on the other side. "God is our refuge and strength, a tested help in times of trouble. And so we need not fear even if the world blows up, and the mountains crumble into the sea. Let the oceans roar and foam; let the mountains tremble! There is a river of joy flowing through the city of our God — the sacred home of the God above all gods. God himself is living in that city; therefore it stands unmoved despite the turmoil everywhere. He will not delay his help" (Psalm 46:1-5).

Now that's an "all-around" Father — one who cares and is readily available to help from any direction. The only one who can hinder his power to help is *you*. He won't force his direction, peace, guidance, protection, or comfort on anyone. But how foolish to have all that assistance so near and try to make it on your own!

Check this. "The steps of good men are directed by the Lord. He delights in each step they take. If they fall it isn't fatal, for the Lord holds them with his hand" (Psalm 37:23, 24).

Here is the testimony of a man who had known the Lord a long time and has seen many miracles performed by him. "I have been young and now I am old. And in all my years I have never seen the Lord forsake a man who loves him; nor have I seen the children of the godly go hungry. Instead, the godly are able to be generous with their gifts and loans to others, and their children are a blessing. So if you want an eternal home, leave your evil, low-down ways and live good lives. For the Lord loves justice and fairness; he will never abandon his people. They will be kept safe forever; but all who love wickedness shall perish" (Psalm 37:25-28).

What to do today:

Just revel (rejoice, frolic, luxuriate) in all God is doing for you! Recognize him all around you and draw on his mighty promises to help you. Read over the ways his love surrounds you and then read them to someone you love.

12

NO PIE IN THE SKY

You have no doubt picked up a few spiritual bruises and realize now that the Christian life is tough as well as tender in this world of overrated pleasures and underrated treasures.

Yes, the "pie in the sky" may have plopped in your eye. The neat little chorus about never being lonely again is a little hard to sing after a siege of loneliness.

And how about depression and anger and other ditches you slipped into? Is God going to protect you from all problems and smooth out all the rough places? No! Just as he did not make an easy earthly life for his Son. But he will go through every situation with you, and he will give all the strength and wisdom you ask him for. Then you'll experience the joy of victory.

One of the most popular chapters in the Bible, Psalm 23, assures you of God's constant care and comfort all through life.

"Because the Lord is my Shepherd, I have everything I need! He lets me rest in the meadow grass and leads me beside the quiet streams. He restores my failing health. He helps me do what honors him the most. Even when walking through the dark valley of death I will not be afraid, for you are close beside me, guarding, and guiding all the way. You provide delicious food for me in the presence of my enemies. You have welcomed me as your guest; blessings overflow! Your goodness and unfailing kindness shall be with me all of my life, and afterwards I will live with you forever in your home."

Let's look at that great psalm a little closer. Notice, he promises everything you *need*, not want. He knows best — do you fully trust him yet? He knows you need an "out" now and then, and he won't let you be tempted more than you can stand. (1 Corinthians 10:13)

I found out about his comfort in the "dark valley of death" when my mother died. Added strength and comfort were given as he promised — just when I needed them.

Jesus once told his disciples that he had "meat to eat that you don't know about." He banqueted on spiritual nourishment from his Father while ungodly people tried to satisfy their moral appetites on garbage.

Some friends of mine passed up lucrative jobs and secure careers to be missionaries. They heard about a very primitive tribe and tried to reach them for Christ, aware of the possibility of death. One of them wrote, "He is no fool who loses what he can not keep (his life) to gain what he cannot lose (eternal reward)." All of them were killed. The world would call their martyrdom "a waste," but those guys carefully counted the cost and gladly paid the price. Besides glorifying God, their sacrifice caused the murderous tribe to be changed eternally through Christ.

What to do today:

Count the cost of being a Christian. Recognize there are no pie-in-the-sky-fantasies such as the end of trouble and sorrow. And tell your Father that since you've come this far you're going all the way with him. Hang tough — you're growing!

13

GET TOUGH

It's about time to flex and use the spiritual muscles you've been developing. Remember, the Christian life is a distance marathon, not a short sprint! It isn't a matter of finishing ahead of someone else but of finishing — and right on course.

Some Christians go blasting down the track of life and stay right on course to a strong finish. Super! But some stumble after leaving the starting line and spend a long time going nowhere. Others get faked into taking a "short-cut" and we don't see them again.

Read the following Bible verse out loud with your name in the blanks. "So _____ runs straight to the goal with purpose in every step. _____ fights to win. _____'s not just shadow-boxing or playing around" (1 Corinthians 9:26).

To accomplish this feat of faithfulness, you're going to need plenty of strength. By now you're aware that you can't progress on your own, so it's time to improve your diet and increase your exercise. "You will never be able to eat solid spiritual food and understand the deeper things of God's Word until you become better Christians and learn right from wrong by practicing doing right" (Hebrews 5:14).

Now that you're getting it all together, your timing and reflexes will begin to improve. You'll sense from within

— by the Holy Spirit — what is right — so practice it. Paul says: "I want to remind you that your strength must come from the Lord's mighty power within you" (Ephesians 6:10).

Don't even think about past failures — or chickening out. Gut it out! It's going to get better and better. If you've tried and failed the last twelve days, forget it! Tell God you're sorry, get the verse back up in the mirror, use your head about what you do and who you run with, and get back on the course. "We are praying, too, that you will be filled with his mighty, glorious strength so that you can keep going no matter what happens — always full of the joy of the Lord and always thankful to the Father who has made us fit to share all the wonderful things that belong to those who live in the kingdom of light" (Colossians 1:11, 12).

What to do today:

Take a minute to determine where you are on the course. You will tend to be pessimistic and hard on yourself. Don't! Remember you're not yet two weeks old in the Lord. But don't excuse laziness or expect results without effort.

Pray this prayer a few times today. Be sure to make it your personal expression and believe with all your heart that God hears and cares.

"Dear Father — I know you know who this is. I'm a very new member of your family and I'm not strong yet. But I want to be! Forgive me where I've failed when I haven't even tried. Be patient with me, Father: I really mean to honor you and please you. Thank you for giving me eternal life. In Jesus' name I pray. Amen."

14

DON'T DEFEAT YOURSELF

Probably the major cause of young Christians slipping back into old ways is "old friends." You know you can't do wrong things and expect to grow spiritually, and you should know there are lots of temptations when you associate with the "old gang." So if you are serious about following Christ, don't defeat yourself by taking up with the people and places that messed up your life before. That makes about as much sense as a guy headed home from the TB ward kissing everyone good-bye so they wouldn't think he was too good for them.

Your old friends will respect you more if you admit you can't handle the things that dragged you down. And they don't really expect you to return though they would be glad to share their misery. The wisest man who ever lived wrote: "Be with wise men and become wise. Be with evil men and become evil" (Proverbs 13:20).

So what am I saying — you should abandon your old friends and ignore them? Definitely not! If you have the courage to tell them that you've received Christ, do it. But tell them individually if you get the opportunity. Everybody in a gang wears a mask for the benefit of others, but alone they are more likely to respond honestly to your witness.

Explain how much your new experience with Christ means. Read them the first few pages of this book if you think it will help. Let them know you want them to check it out for themselves, and invite them to a meeting where the gospel will be presented. Don't criticize; keep it positive! And let them know you sincerely care.

The Apostle James put the matter very clearly. "I say it again, that if your aim is to enjoy the evil pleasures of the unsaved world, you cannot also be a friend of God, or what do you think the Scripture means when it says that the Holy Spirit, whom God has placed within us, watches over us with tender jealousy? But he gives us more and more strength to stand against all such evil longings. As the Scripture says, God gives strength to the humble, but sets himself against the proud and haughty. So give yourself humbly to God. Resist the devil and he will flee from you. And when you draw close to God, God will draw close to you" (James 4:4-7).

What to do today:

Make the break with people, places, or habits that weaken you and tie you to past sin.

You've been *born again*! You're a royal child of God! You're a winner, not a loser — unless you defeat yourself!

15

YOUR BIBLE

You've no doubt noticed that I've used the Bible as the guidebook for Christian living. That's not my idea. Jesus' friend the Apostle James was way ahead of me — strengthening Christians in the faith by frequent use of "the Scripture" (James 4:4-6). No one has ever become a strong Christian without knowing and obeying the Bible.

The Bible is the *Word of God*. He gave it to us so we could clearly know what he is like and how we can please him. And there are over 3,000 promises recorded in the Scriptures — many of which apply to us. Someone has said the Bible is God's love letter to us.

I heard a story about a college girl who took a course that required extensive reading in a textbook she found exceedingly boring. At the same time she was dating a young professor from a nearby university. Before long she fell in love and then learned her fiancé was the author of the miserable textbook.

That same evening she read it late into the night. Unbelievably, she could hardly put it down! Had the textbook been changed? No, but she had! She was in love with the author. And what he wrote was now personal and meaningful.

You've been changed, too! Now that you know the Author of life itself, read his words with confidence and love. His words and your faith make an overpowering combination for daily living. Plant these words in your heart:

"The reverence and fear of God are basic to all wisdom. Knowing God results in every other kind of understanding" (Proverbs 9:10).

"All he does is just and good, and all his laws are right, for they are formed from truth and goodness, and stand firm forever" (Psalm 111:7).

"Obey me and live! Guard my words as your most precious possession. Write them down, and also keep them deep within your heart" (Proverbs 7:2, 3).

"These things that were written in the Scriptures so long ago are to teach us patience and encourage us" (Romans 15:4a).

"The whole Bible was given us by inspiration from God and is useful to teach us what is true and to make us realize what is wrong in our lives; it straightens us out and helps us to do what is right. It is God's way of making us well prepared at every point, fully equipped to do good to everyone" (2 Timothy 3:16, 17).

"For no prophecy recorded in Scripture was ever thought up by the prophet himself. It was the Holy Spirit within these godly men who gave them true messages from God" (2 Peter 1:20, 21).

What to do today:

Get your Bible and read a few verses before and after these verses.

Begin the habit of letting God speak to you through the Bible every day. Choose a time when you're unhurried, alone, and uninterrupted. You may have to work at it, but it's worth it!

Here are a few chapters for you to begin reading. Underline verses in your Bible that bless you and blast you.

The whole book of John
2 Corinthians 5
Romans 8
Galatians 5
1 Corinthians 13

PRAYER

"Now I lay me down to sleep . . ."

"Our Father which art in heaven . . ."

That's the limit of some Christians' prayer vocabulary. And they say they "love the Lord"!

If I recited the same words to my wife every time I spoke to her, she would be justified in doubting my love as well as my sanity. She might also be justified in denting my skull!

Our Father loves to hear us pray — really *pray*. The Apostle John revealed part of the meaning of prayer in his vision of heaven: " . . . and golden vials filled with incense — the prayers of God's people" (Revelation 5: 8b). God actually preserves our prayers — isn't that fantastic!

Prayer is important to you too. Your Father is an attentive listener. And today we need someone to listen. Everybody and his grandmother are interrupting to give us the inside scoop or formula for success. If you've had an accident, operation, or moon walk, they've had a better one or "know how you feel." "One-up your buddy" is the slogan of the day.

So how refreshing it is to get quiet and talk to the One who listens, understands, and cares. And answers!

You say, "That's fine, but I don't know how to pray!" God knows about that problem and has done something about it. What follows will bless you. Read it carefully.

"And in the same way — by our faith — the Holy Spirit helps us with our daily problems and in our praying. For we don't even know what we should pray for, nor how to pray as we should; but the Holy Spirit prays for us with such feeling that it cannot be expressed in words. And the Father who knows all hearts knows, of course, what the Spirit is saying as he pleads for us in harmony with God's own will" (Romans 8:26, 27).

The utterly phenomenal possibilities represented in that promise are overwhelming. I just sat here and reread those verses a few times, and I'm ashamed of myself for getting so busy that I don't take time more often to activate that supernatural power within me.

That's right! We have to turn the "key." Look at the first part of the verse: ". . . by our faith . . ." — the immeasurable power of the Spirit of God responds to our faith in prayer and action.

So don't feel sorry for yourself or make excuses about not knowing how to pray. Tell God you love him, thank him for Jesus, and count on the Holy Spirit praying with you. Don't be anxious about using the "right" words — God is interested in *honest* expression.

"But when you pray, go away by yourself, all alone, and shut the door behind you and pray to your Father secretly, and your Father, who knows your secrets, will reward you" (Matthew 6:6).

"Keep alert and pray. Otherwise temptation will overpower you. For the spirit indeed is willing, but how weak the body is" (Matthew 26:41).

"The earnest prayer of a righteous man has great power and wonderful results" (James 5:16).

These are just a few of the hundreds of verses about prayer in the Bible. Find some others and try them in your life.

Jesus gave a guideline to prayer in Matthew 6, and we read his prayer to his heavenly Father in John 17. Be sure to read this carefully. You'll be thrilled by his concern and love for you.

God isn't a bad-tempered ogre daring you to approach; he is your loving Father and he wants to fellowship with you. So talk to him in the car, at school, and at home. (Better not pray out loud when you're walking down the halls, though, somebody might throw a net over you.) But talk to him. Have the times of prayer behind closed doors, but be spontaneous too. Remember — you love each other!

What to do today:

Get a piece of paper and start a prayer list. Put your name on top, then others you want to pray for. Use this list during your daily quiet time.

See what happens when you activate the great praying power of the Holy Spirit today — by your faith.

Remember too — there are people praying for *you*.

"Don't be weary in prayer; keep at it; watch for God's answers and remember to be thankful when they come" (Colossians 4:2).

17

TEMPTATION

The only people who aren't tempted to do wrong are those whose names are on marble stones. So don't think you're a special target or the pressure is too much to handle. Everyone is tempted. But not everyone has to give in or be plowed under. First of all, realize where temptation comes from and why.

"And remember, when someone wants to do wrong, it is never God who is tempting him, for God never wants to do wrong and never tempts anyone else to do it. Temptation is the pull of man's own evil thoughts and wishes. These evil thoughts lead to evil actions and afterwards to the death penalty from God. So don't be misled, dear brothers" (James 1:13-16).

Now that you know the "where" and "why," you might want to check chapter 14 again: "Don't Defeat Yourself." We're all on ego trips of varying degrees, but don't let your ingrown eyeballs affect your intelligence. Don't put the blame on "the world," "that's just the way I am," "my friends," "our society," etc. Don't hang around infection! When you see or hear something that could lead to wrongdoing, quickly ask for help. Every second it lies unchallenged in your mind it spreads and decays.

"But remember this — the wrong desires that come into your life aren't anything new and different. Many others have faced exactly the same problems before you.

And no temptation is irresistible. You can trust God to keep the temptation from becoming so strong that you can't stand up against it, for he has promised this and will do what he says. He will show you how to escape temptation's power so that you can bear up patiently against it" (1 Corinthians 10:13).

If you really believe and apply that verse to your life you'll become a *powerful* Christian.

You may have noticed that we're getting into tougher spiritual exercises. But to stay on course and keep going you'll have to know your enemy and how to beat him. It's worth it. "Happy is the man who doesn't give in and do wrong when he is tempted. For afterwards he will get as his reward the crown of life that God has promised those who love him" (James 1:12).

What to do today:

First, write out the words of 1 Corinthians 10:13. Then list some people or places that represent temptation to you. Be honest! (Burn the list later.)

Next, either admit to God you love your old habits and ways too much and you've decided to remain spiritually retarded, or tell him you trust him and his judgment about what's best for you and you'll back away from these so you can grow spiritually.

18

YOUR MIND

Your mind is the control room of your body. You can't talk, move, or think intelligently without your mind's cooperation. Whatever you feel — heat, cold, pain, etc., — goes first to the mind for identification and assignment of a suitable response. Whatever emotion you feel — love, anger, happiness, — does the same. In other words, there isn't a single thing we do that isn't programmed first through that marvelous "computer" on our shoulders.

So the real battle of life takes place in your mind. Every temptation must first be processed there. All decisions will first be decided in your brain. Like the seed that produces the mighty oak tree, it progresses from a thought to a deed to a habit to character to destiny — all beginning in the mind.

"Above all else guard your affections. For they influence everything else in your life" (Proverbs 4:23).

Think of yourself like this:

  body
  soul
  spirit

The body is the vehicle for movement, instrument for action, and image for identification.

The soul or "heart" encompasses the mind which thinks, the emotions which "feel," and the will which decides.

The spirit is the "inner man," the God-conscious life which became the abode of the Holy Spirit when you became a child of God by faith in Christ.

The Holy Spirit seeks to express his goodness and power through your mind and conduct, but he is opposed at times by your selfish and impure thoughts. If we allow those thoughts to remain in our minds or produce actions, we grieve the Spirit. Said the Apostle Paul, "Don't cause the Holy Spirit sorrow by the way you live" (Ephesians 4:30).

"Live no longer as the unsaved do, for they are blinded and confused. Their closed hearts are full of darkness; they are far away from the life of God because they have shut their minds against him, and they cannot understand his ways. They don't care anymore about right and wrong and have given themselves over to impure ways. They stop at nothing, being driven by their evil minds and reckless lusts" (Ephesians 4:17-19).

There are a lot of philosophers, psychiatrists, and pushers who want to change our minds, blow our minds, vitalize them, and expand them. We are forever being challenged to "use our heads"; we're mind-oriented. But with all the ideas and philosophies come fewer answers and more problems. The real answer must be deeper than the mind!

The answer is in the spiritual realm. Man's mind is crippled by sin, and he cannot understand God's truth until his spirit is linked to the Spirit of God.

"The man who isn't a Christian can't understand and

accept these thoughts from God which the Holy Spirit teaches us. They sound foolish to him, because only those who have the Holy Spirit within them can understand what he teaches. Others just can't take it in. But the spiritual man has insight into everything, and that bothers and baffles the man of the world, who can't understand him at all. . . . But strange as it seems, we Christians actually do have within us a portion of the very thoughts and mind of Christ" (1 Corinthians 2:14-16).

"So what about these wise men, these scholars, these brilliant debaters of this world's great affairs? God has made them all look foolish, and shown their wisdom to be useless nonsense" (1 Corinthians 1:20).

But notice the contrast as you read this verse: "He will keep in perfect peace all those who trust in him, whose thoughts turn often to the Lord!" (Isaiah 26:3). So guard your mind — and then your conversation and conduct will please God and fill your life with good things.

What to do today:

"Don't worry about anything; instead, pray about everything; tell God your needs and don't forget to thank him for his answers. If you do this you will experience God's peace, which is far more wonderful than the human mind can understand. His peace will keep your thoughts and your hearts quiet and at rest as you trust in Christ Jesus" (Philippians 4:6, 7).

"Fix your thoughts on what is true and good and right. Think about things that are pure and lovely, and dwell on the fine, good things in others. Think about all you can praise God for and be glad about" (Philippians 4:8b).

Begin practicing this positive spiritual thinking now. Don't let a critical, vengeful, or bitter thought poison your mind today; throw it out fast. Remember it is the Holy Spirit who renews and purifies your mind (2 Timothy 1:7).

19

YOUR FAITH

It's time to "step on the scales" and see if you're gaining any spiritual weight. You probably won't see as much improvement as you'd like, but others are aware of the "new you" if you've been following the spiritual diet and exercise schedule.

The new you hasn't been so reluctant to say "I'm sorry" or "I was wrong." You think a little more about others lately; you try to eliminate harmful, negative, and fearful thoughts; you share insight during a conversation instead of criticism; you surprise your family by reacting differently than you used to.

Congratulations! You're doing great. After all, what would anyone expect of a two-week-old child! Be sure not to get down on yourself and expect too much too soon.

As this is a critical stage in your spiritual development, I want to give you a key to unending growth and happiness. If you use this key, the barriers that usually block people will become doors to you, and the hassles that frustrate others will be bridges for you.

The key is *faith*. God says you can't please him without it (Hebrews 11:6).

"What is faith? It is the confident assurance that something we want is going to happen. It is the certainty that what we hope for is waiting for us, even though we cannot see it up ahead" (Hebrews 11:1).

You use faith a lot in everyday life. For example, you trust in medicine, a car, electricity, and other things you don't fully understand. Your active faith in God will deepen your prayers, strengthen your confidence in God, and embolden your service. As your faith is exercised, the results will multiply.

Remember the woman who touched Jesus' robe (Matthew 9:20)? Jesus said, "Your faith has healed you."

In Mark 2 we read about four men who took a house apart to get their sick friend to Jesus. "Seeing their faith," Jesus healed the needy man.

Jesus is the same yesterday, today, and forever, as we are told in Hebrews 13:8. He still responds to faith — your faith.

How much faith do you have? That's the faith to act on — right now! Faith grows as you use it, and as you become better acquainted with the Rewarder of faith. Jesus gave this encouragement:

"If you hardhearted, sinful men know how to give good gifts to your children, won't your Father in heaven even more certainly give good gifts to those who ask him for them?" (Matthew 7:11). Since one of his "good gifts" is faith, ask for *that* if you lack it!

What to do today:

How are you doing with the verse in the mirror? Don't foul up here! Filtering that verse through your mind is very important.

Take ten minutes today to read Hebrews 11 and underline the word "faith" every time you find it. I recommend *The Living Bible* for your reading (*The Way*, in paperback edition); it's paraphrased for easy reading.

OOPS — AGAIN!

Whether you have been flying along and suddenly crashed or have been stumbling rather consistently on the Christian course, no doubt you have heard a whisper like this: "Give up, dummy! This life isn't for you. You can't cut this kind of action. Look how you mess up all the time. And who wants to be a goody-goody anyway?"

That's Satan's voice — and he's a liar. It costs you plenty every time you listen to a liar. If this has happened to you, get 1 John 1:9 up in the mirror again.

"But God seems so far away," you say. "Like he gave up on me."

That reminds me of the middle-aged couple driving behind a jacked-up Chevy in which guy and girl were both sitting behind the steering wheel — two heads, one body. The lady said, "Look at that, Charlie, isn't that nice? Look how they're cuddled beside each other. Remember when we used to ride like that? Whatever happened to us, Charlie? Here we are on *opposite sides* of the car." Charlie gripped the steering wheel a little harder and said, "*I* didn't move!"

If God seems irrelevant or distant, guess who moved? Not God! By now you know how to stay close — so do it! Don't make excuses or look for short cuts. Tough it out! Nobody has outgiven God, and you won't be the first.

"Obey God because you are his children; don't slip back into your old ways — doing evil because you knew no better. But be holy now in everything you do, just as the Lord is holy, who invited you to be his child" (1 Peter 1:14, 15).

To be really victorious in the Christian life, you need to know five things that God won't do for you — that's right, he won't do *for you*:

1. Give yourself humbly to God;
2. Resist the devil so he will flee from you;
3. Draw close to God so he will draw close to you;
4. Wash your hands of sin (that means get rid of obvious sin in your life);
5. Fill your heart with God alone to be pure and true.

These things were written by James to *Christians* — to you and me. *We* must do these things because we love and trust God.

God is going to hold on to you, even after you sin. He loves you even when you hurt him. You may let go of him, but he'll never let go of you.

As in every family, my children have disobeyed me many times. I may make them uncomfortable and somewhat miserable for awhile — because to ignore their disobedience would be to show I don't love them. And the consequences become more severe for them if they get away with wrong. So because I sincerely love them and want them to live happy, fulfilled lives, I direct them in the right ways.

If I care enough to do that, how much more your heavenly Father wants the best for you. If you try to play games with him, you'll lose every time. When you've sinned, admit it! Don't justify or excuse yourself. And if he puts the pressure on you, don't get mad; look for the reason and thank him. Remember: "We know that all that happens to us is working for good if we love God and are fitting into his plans" (Romans 8:28).

What to do today:

Thumb back through the preceeding chapters and reread chapters 15, 12, and 9. Look for some reasons why you stumbled, if you did.

Go into a quiet room alone and tell God you're honestly sorry for your failures. Tell him you love him and ask him for strength to do the five things *you* must do.

Read David's prayer of remorse and repentance in Psalm 51.

YOUR PERSONALITY

Have you ever said, "That's just the way I am; I can't help it"? In a way that's right, but usually it's a cop-out. It's easier to ask other people to adjust to our ways than for us to change in order to please them. And have you noticed how much easier it is to get along with some people than with others? The reasons for all this are very interesting — and actually quite simple.

Each human personality has a combination of characteristics, but there seem to be four distinct personality-temperament types. Most people appear to be dominated by characteristics in one temperament and strongly influenced by traits of a second type. See if you can find yourself in the following categories.

Sanguine — is an extroverted optimist. He is emotional and warm. A fast talker who can convince others, he's friendly and has a nice personality. He's fun to be around because he's happy and lives in the present. But he's also impulsive and changeable.

Melancholy — is an introverted pessimist. He is very selective and thorough about life. A deep thinker, his idealism tends to exaggerate the negative. He is careful planner and very conscientious — which may lead him to be critical and suspicious.

If a melancholy type saw two people talking, he would suspect that they were saying something bad about him.

The sanguine in the same situation would think they were admiring him.

Choleric — is a strong-willed, hard-driving person. He sets high goals and works tirelessly to achieve them. He may use people for his own purpose, then ignore them, and is generally unsympathetic — especially with weak or lazy people. He is practical and opportunistic. In emergencies or facing challenges, he is calm, discerning, and confident. Most great leaders are cholerics.

Phlegmatic — is the slow, good-natured person who drives energetic sanguines and cholerics up the wall. He has inner balance and common sense, is a practical and accurate worker. Not very creative, he sees many sides of an issue. A peace lover, he makes a good friend.

Well, did you find yourself? Nobody fits perfectly into any of these temperament types, so we can only classify ourselves in a general way. But perhaps you now realize why certain people and actions attract you and some habits or characteristics of people bug you. This insight was a great help in my life and marriage. I used to think my wife did certain things just to irritate me. It didn't dawn on me that some of my ways bothered her just as much. When we understood the differences in our personality types we found it easier to adjust and please each other.

Your Father, the Creator, made you a certain way, and he doesn't want you to act like a phlegmatic if he made you a sanguine. You have certain characteristics for particular service to God — *but* most good traits have a corresponding weak trait, and the Holy Spirit can develop a balance that will make you a stronger and more compassionate child of God. Recognize the weaknesses of your temperament(s) and seek to strengthen them.

Opposite temperaments do attract — because they complement the strengths possessed by each person. Peter was a far-out sanguine, but his partner, John, was a melancholy. Most good marriages are made up of opposites whose strengths support each other and weaknesses are submerged in mutual love and respect.

Jesus was the only man in whom all the temperaments were perfectly balanced.

Now that you know yourself and others better, you should be more patient and loving. Make your home and relationships more enjoyable by getting to know and care about people.

"And now this word to all of you: You should be like one big happy family, full of sympathy toward each other, loving one another with tender hearts and humble minds. Don't repay evil for evil. Don't snap back at those who say unkind things about you. Instead, pray for God's help for them, for we are to be kind to others, and God will bless us for it. If you want a happy, good life, keep control of your tongue, and guard your lips from telling lies. Turn away from evil and do good. Try to live in peace even if you must run after it to catch and hold it! For the Lord is watching his children, listening to their prayers; but the Lord's face is hard against those who do evil" (1 Peter 3:8-12).

What to do today:

Check your reactions toward people and situations to see if your strengths or weaknesses are responding. Remember that Satan knows your temperament and will tempt you where you're weak. He knows sanguines are impulsive, melancholics are easily depressed, cholerics are self-centered, and phlegmatics give up easily. So be on guard today! Don't forget the "super-temperament" within you — the Holy Spirit — who gives power over every temptation and weakness.

22

TIME TO SHARE

You're three weeks old now in Jesus Christ, and if you have been faithfully progressing, you're aware of spiritual strength and discernment you didn't think were possible. You're also excited about sharing what you've discovered. Some Christians aren't excited about sharing their faith — they have a weak or sickly brand, and it's just as well they don't share that!

So let your Christian convictions control your conduct, then when people ask what makes you tick, tell them! Peter has some counsel for you at this point: "Quietly trust yourself to Christ your Lord and if anybody asks why you believe as you do, be ready to tell him, and do it in a gentle and respectful way" (1 Peter 3:15).

Your confidence will increase as your knowledge and experience increases. In other words, if you've goofed off with the verses in the mirror and haven't memorized any yet, you can't readily answer anybody because you don't know what to say. But if you're excited by living your new life you'll excite others. You don't have to be Billy Graham to get the message across — just prove your words by living Christ's life.

Witnessing is very important to God, Jesus said in Luke 12:8, 9 — "And I assure you of this: I, the Messiah, will publicly honor you in the presence of God's angels if you publicly acknowledge me here on earth as your friend.

But I will deny before the angels those who deny me here among men."

Paul explained the high responsibility of Christian witness: "For we speak as messengers from God, trusted by him to tell the truth; we change his message not one bit to suit the taste of those who hear it; for we serve God alone, who examines our hearts' deepest thoughts" (1 Thessalonians 2:4).

By now I hope you realize you are the carriers of eternal life. If people are going to find Christ, they'll find him through Christians who care enough to share. How you do it isn't very important; just tell what Jesus means to you. It's the natural thing for a happy Christian. "For it is by believing in his heart that a man becomes right with God and with his mouth he tells others of his faith, confirming his salvation" (Romans 10:10).

Memorize these verses, and you'll have one answer for those who ask. "I am not ashamed of this good news about Christ! It is God's powerful method of bringing all who believe it to heaven. . . . This good news tells us that God makes us ready for heaven — makes us right in God's sight — when we put our faith and trust in Christ to save us. This is accomplished from start to finish by faith" (Romans 1:16a, 17).

What to do today:

Pray for the Spirit's guidance to share your faith with someone who doesn't know Christ, then speak up — like someone spoke up to you.

23

TWO MASTERS

As long as you breathe, you're going to be aware of your old self fighting with the new you. If you surrender to old ways, you are again serving Satan, your former master. Though he has lost you to Christ, he has not given up trying to injure and incapacitate you.

Probably the "disease" that has deformed more young Christians than any other is materialism. Many Christians trust God except for money and things. They must think God doesn't care about money. But listen to Matthew — "Don't store up treasures here on earth where they can erode away or may be stolen. Store them in heaven where they will never lose their value, and are safe from thieves. If your profits are in heaven your heart will be there too. You cannot serve two masters: God and money" (6:19, 24).

Now, don't get the idea I'm going to ask you to take a vow of poverty or sell everything and take to the hills. It's just that God knows the glitter of gold can blind you to the really important things of life — primarily, that of knowing him better and serving him well.

Actually, God is a jealous Father — in the best sense. He wants to give you good things and prosper you, but he is watching out for your *eternal* welfare and if that will be enhanced by supplying you with lots of money you'll have it! But wealth ruins more people than it helps.

And you needn't worry about lacking necessities. "Your heavenly Father already knows perfectly well that you need them, and he will give them to you if you give him first place in your life and live as he wants you to" (Matthew 6:33).

The man considered the wisest and the richest of all said a few things about money. "Trust in your money and down you go. Trust in God and flourish as a tree!" (Proverbs 11:28). "Your riches won't help you on judgment day. Only righteousness counts then" (Proverbs 11:4).

Jesus asked bluntly: "And how does a man benefit if he gains the whole world and loses his soul in the process? For is anything worth more than his soul?" (Mark 8:36, 37).

Be very careful, as you mature spiritually, that you consider the priorities in your life. Without faith it's impossible to please God, and one of the most important steps of faith is your trusting him with money. Invest your money gifts in a way that will help people to know Jesus.

What to do today:

Begin to tithe. Take 10 percent off the top of your income and get it working for eternal dividends. Later, as God prospers you, give more. "But remember this — if you give little, you will get little. A farmer who plants just a few seeds will get only a small crop, but if he plants much, he will reap much. Everyone must make up his own mind as to how much he should give. Don't force anyone to give more than he really wants to, for cheerful givers are the ones God prizes. God is able to make it up to you by giving you everything you need and more, so that there will not only be enough for your own needs, but plenty left over to give joyfully to others" (2 Corinthians 9:6-8).

24

MEMO FOR HUSBANDS

God wants Christian husbands to be well informed of their privileges and responsibilities. "For a husband is in charge of his wife in the same way Christ is in charge of his body, the church. He gave his very life to take care of it and be its Savior!" (Ephesians 5:23).

All direction for our bodies comes through our minds (Chapter 18). As the husband is the *head* of the home, just as Christ is Head of the Church, the direction for wives and children comes from the Christian husband-father. When he places high priority on spiritual things — praying and living by faith — wives and children will be constructively influenced and God will be honored in the family.

God requires that husbands take good care of their wives. "You husbands must be careful of your wives, being thoughtful of their needs and honoring them as the weaker sex. Remember that you and your wife are partners in receiving God's blessings, and if you don't treat her as you should, your prayers will not get ready answers" (1 Peter 3:7).

"And you husbands, show the same kind of love to your wives as Christ showed to the Church when he died for her" (Ephesians 5:25).

If your wife is not yet a child of God, you can see how imperative it is for you to be patient and kind in showing the love of God. Don't let her reject Christ because she can't see him in you.

Be the spiritual leader in your home. Don't send your children to Sunday school and church — take them! And there is a godly discipline with godly results. "Don't keep on scolding and nagging your children, making them angry and resentful. Rather, bring them up with the loving discipline the Lord himself approves, with suggestions and godly advice" (Ephesians 6:4).

What to do today:

Work at being patient with your wife and children. Tell God you accept your responsibilities as head of the home and you desire his help.

25

A WORD TO WIVES

Although the man is responsible to God as the head of the home, the role of wife and mother is one of the most influential in life. She has a great deal to do with her husband's and family's success, as Solomon declared. "A worthy wife is her husband's joy and crown; the other kind corrodes his strength and tears down everything he does" (Proverbs 12:4).

Now that you're a Christian, you have the potential for channeling God's blessings to every member of your family. Whereas you formerly lived for yourself — as every unregenerated person does — you now have the incentive and power from the Holy Spirit to live for others. This Christlike life is very convincing to a non-Christian husband, as Peter says, "Wives, fit in with your husbands' plans; for then if they refuse to listen when you talk to them about the Lord, they will be won by your respectful, pure behavior. Your godly lives will speak to them better than any words" (1 Peter 3:1, 2).

God's Word reveals his plan for leadership in the family. Successful marriages are not 50-50, but 100-100, each giving 100 percent. "You wives must submit to your husbands' leadership in the same way you submit to the Lord. So you wives must willingly obey your husbands in everything, just as the Church obeys Christ" (Ephesians 5:21, 22, 24). Husbands do not have the wisdom of Christ, but they have God-ordained authority in the Christian home.

A mother's influence on children is deep and lasting. Let them sense your faith and confidence in God as you read the Bible and pray with them. Train them in faith by your example. Be fair and firm in your discipline. Don't leave it all for Dad when he arrives home — lest he become a tyrant in the eyes of his children.

Don't compete with children by arguing; you have the responsibility of making decisions because you're the parent, not because of superior eloquence or lung power. But let growing children make more and more guided decisions, and be willing to admit it when you're wrong.

I spoke to an adult-youth group on parent-teen relations and later a mother shared this experience with me. On the way home her sixteen-year-old daughter commented: "Well, Mother, I hope you learned something tonight." The mother said she got so angry she could hardly see and started to rebuke this "disrespect." Suddenly she remembered something I had said and swallowed her anger. Finally, she said, "Yes, honey, I did learn something tonight and I realize I've often been wrong. I'm going to try to be a better mother." There was no answer for minutes from the girl in the back seat, then with a sob the daughter put her arms around her mother and cried like a baby. She admitted her selfishness and critical spirit and asked forgiveness. Needless to say, real communication was restored and a new relationship established.

That happened because a woman acted maturely instead of satisfying her anger or injured pride. She obeyed the Holy Spirit and the results were deeply gratifying. "A soft answer turns away wrath, but harsh words cause quarrels" (Proverbs 15:1). "Be patient and you will finally win, for a soft tongue can break hard bones" (Proverbs 25:15).

Mother-wife, the spirit of your home depends primarily on you. If you're impatient and demanding, the atmosphere will be tense. If you're cheerful and considerate, your home will be enjoyable and its members relaxed. And your husband and children will admire and praise you.

If love makes the world go 'round, our globe is in danger of stopping. Real love is scarce in today's society, and Christian mothers can do a lot about this lack. Demonstrate real love, such as is described in 1 Corinthians 13. "If you love someone you will be loyal to him no matter what the cost. You will always believe in him, always expect the best of him, and always stand your ground in defending him" (13:7).

And don't be fooled by "women's liberation" and the extreme feminist movement. Their demands are contrary to what God says will make a woman happy and fulfilled. Since he created woman, you can trust him and his ways.

What to do today:

Find an occasion to say something encouraging to every member of your family. Read 1 Corinthians 13 to your husband and tell him that's your goal, with God's help.

DEAR SONS AND DAUGHTERS

The "in" thing with some sons and daughters is to say, "My parents are weird"; "My home's a bummer"; "Everything is establishment"; and split! That action is a cop-out. Things don't go their way — so they run. Others don't agree — so they disappear.

There might be a slim possibility that a fraction of the blame for a lousy home situation belongs to the complainer! Every record has a flip side — if parents won't listen, kids can listen a little harder. If parents won't discuss problems without arguing, kids can act their *parents'* age — and watch it blow their minds! Kids who yell back or leave confirm their parents' opinions and make things worse.

Some kids who don't know Jesus could care less about their parents and their homes. But Christians are different. "Children, obey your parents" is God's command, and it pays off. "Honor your father and mother. This is the first of God's Ten Commandments that ends with a promise. And this is the promise: that if you honor your father and mother, yours will be a long life, full of blessing" (Ephesians 6:1-3).

Your heavenly Father considers the home and family important. He knows that obeying and honoring parents is the toughest discipline of some young Christians' lives. It can be accepted as a challenge — for Jesus' sake. If you intend to try, it will help you to tell your parents — by putting yourself on the spot and signaling for the Holy Spirit's help.

"And now this word to all of you; You should be like one big happy family, full of sympathy toward each other, loving one another with tender hearts and humble minds. Don't repay evil for evil. Don't snap back at those who say unkind things about you. Instead pray for God's help for them, for we are to be kind to others, and God will bless us for it. If you want a happy, good life, keep control of your tongue and guard your lips from telling lies" (1 Peter 3:8-10).

What to do today:

If you can, tell your parents you love them and are grateful to them. Ask the Holy Spirit to enable you to go the whole day without any smart mouth or arguing. Read 1 Peter 3:8-10 over five times.

27

FORGIVENESS

You are growing in spiritual maturity now, so I want to alert you to a principle that is a "must" for a productive Christian. It's *forgiveness!* If you read Jesus' words in Matthew 18:21-34, you'll get an idea how essential this is. I'm sure Peter got the message: forgive 490 times, and if you haven't got the habit of forgiving by then you're hopelessly childish.

An unforgiving spirit will stunt your growth by closing off an area of your life to God. This sin advances the devil's cause, as Paul said. "A further reason for forgiveness is to keep from being outsmarted by Satan; for we know what he is trying to do" (2 Corinthians 2: 11). Once you have truly received Christ as Savior, Satan cannot control you but he can tempt you. If he can get you to watch Christians' inconsistencies and failures, he can taunt you about the reality of all you've believed in.

The way to handle this subtle attack is to *keep your focus on Jesus,* not on Christians. Don't try to figure out why they do this or don't do that. They are not your model; Jesus Christ is. And he tells you to forgive endlessly.

In Matthew 6 Jesus gave an example of prayer to his disciples. Among other expressions he directed them to pray: "Forgive us our sins, just as we have forgiven those who have sinned against us" (6:12). Make sure you can honestly pray those words.

What to do today:

If you are looking for a way to "pay somebody back" or get revenge, ask God to forgive you and to give you love to forgive the offender. This is one of the "good gifts" your heavenly Father will give you.

GOD'S WILL

Now that we're just a couple of days from the end of the month, let's look back. If you've made even a half effort, you'll be surprised and delighted at what you see. You've really come a long way, haven't you? Of course you aren't a Moses or Paul yet, but you're not a Jezebel or Judas either. You're growing!

And with that realization will come a more determined effort to continue doing God's will. You'll find that knowing and doing his will gets easier all the time. Jesus said, "Come to me and I will give you rest — all of you who work so hard beneath a heavy yoke. Wear my yoke — for it fits perfectly — and let me teach you; for I am gentle and humble, and you shall find rest for your souls; for I give you only light burdens" (Matthew 11: 28-30).

You have already heard or will hear many references to "God's will." Some make it sound like a mystery. Others suppose it to be "whatever happens, man," and take a fatalistic, neutral position on everything. But it's neither of these! It is a beautifully intricate plan that God has worked out *for your benefit* and happiness. (See Ephesians 1:11.)

Paul wanted the Colossians to know God's will, and he spelled it out very clearly for them in the first chapter, verses 9 and 10. "So ever since we first heard about you we have kept on praying and asking God to help you understand what he wants you to do; asking him to make you wise about spiritual things; and asking that the way you live will always please the Lord and honor him, so that you will always be doing good, kind things for others, while all the time you are learning to know God better and better." Let me break it down even more; this is God's will for you:

1. Your conduct will please *him*. A noble child of royalty (which you are) has high and challenging responsibilities because of the close relationship to the King.
2. Look for ways to be kind to others — and when they ask why, share your faith and love in Christ.
3. Continue to grow up in spiritual understanding and strength. Do this with a balance of quiet devotion (where you worship and fellowship with your Father) and some hard disciplines that produce spiritual muscle. There are some of both described in the preceding chapters.

"We are praying, too, that you will be filled with his mighty, glorious strength so that you can keep going no matter what happens — always full of joy in the Lord" (Colossians 1:11). That is God's will, too, and this strength and joy in his will depends on your obedience and steady fellowship with God.

Finally, it is God's will that you know the gifts the Holy Spirit gives so you can be more effective by using your gift. That's right! *Your* gift. Each of us is given at least one gift and it's up to us to recognize it and use it.

Here's a list of the gifts in 1 Corinthians 12 (take a

few minutes to read the whole chapter so you understand the setting and context).

1. The ability to give wise advice
2. Studying and teaching
3. Special faith
4. Power to heal the sick
5. Power to do miracles
6. Power to prophesy and preach
7. Power to discern evil spirits
8. Ability to speak in languages one has never learned
9. Ability to interpret the languages

"It is the same and only Holy Spirit who gives all these gifts and powers, deciding which each one of us should have" (1 Corinthians 12:11).

A similar list in the same chapter gives:

1. Apostles
2. Prophets — those who preach God's Word
3. Teachers
4. Those who do miracles
5. Those who have the gift of healing
6. Those who can help others
7. Those who can get others to work together
8. Those who speak in languages they have never learned.

A brief list in Ephesians 4 includes:

1. Apostles
2. Those who can preach well
3. Special ability in winning people to Christ
4. Caring for God's people — leading and teaching them in the ways of God.

Finally, Romans 12 instructs us how to use our gifts.

"God has given each of us the ability to do certain things well. So if God has given you the ability to prophesy, then prophesy whenever you can — as often as your faith is strong enough to receive a message from God.

"If your gift is that of serving others, serve them well.

"If you are a teacher, do a good job of teaching.

"If you are a preacher, see to it that your sermons are strong and helpful.

"If God has given you money, be generous in helping others with it.

"If God has given you administrative ability and put you in charge of the work of others, take your responsibility seriously.

"Those who offer comfort to the sorrowing should do so with Christian cheer" (12:6-8).

Listen to Paul's advice to young Timothy. "Be sure to use the abilities God has given you. . . . Put these abilities to work; throw yourself into your tasks so that everyone may notice your improvement and progress. Keep a close watch on all you do and think. Stay true to what is right and God will bless you and use you to help others" (1 Timothy 4:14-16). Paul affirms in Ephesians 4:7 — "Christ has given each of us special abilities. . . ."

What to do today:

Spend some concentrated time in prayer and study about these gifts. Ask God to help you to know yours. Don't wait for a voice in the night or a brick from the blue to certify the message: pick one you feel may be yours and put it to work.

And work at being kind to someone today.

WHAT'S IN IT FOR ME?

It sounds like a paradox or a conflict of interest to ask a question like "What's in it for me?" when we consider the results of living for Christ. There's a great deal "in it" for us when we obey Jesus' admonition to "lay up treasure in heaven" (Matthew 6:20). But this treasure is gained only through unselfish action, and it glorifies God as well as benefits us.

Reward has always been a motivating factor in the family of God — not in man-made religions that threaten punishment if you *don't* do certain things and perform certain rituals. Spiritual rewards are the supernatural results of obeying God's laws. If we mess around in the world and never grow up spiritually we cheat ourselves, but the immeasurable riches of God are ours if we live for him.

"Prove me now, says the Lord of hosts, if I will not open the windows of heaven, and pour out a blessing, that there will not be room enough to receive it" (Malachi 3:10). In other words, you can't outgive God! But it's very worthwhile to try!

To encourage you to strive for the best, look at these five crowns you can win from Christ's hand — in addition to the good things you'll receive down here.

1. *The incorruptible crown.* "To win the contest you must deny yourselves many things that would keep

you from doing your best. An athlete goes to all this trouble just to win a blue ribbon or a silver cup, but we do it for a heavenly (incorruptible) reward that never disappears" (1 Corinthians 9:25). You've got to fight for this one; stay on the course and keep on truckin'.

2. *The crown of rejoicing.* "For what is it we live for, that gives us hope and joy and is our proud reward and crown. It is you! Yes, you will bring us much joy as we stand together before our Lord Jesus Christ when he comes back again" (1 Thessalonians 2:19, 20). This one's for soul-winners; you can win this by sharing your faith. Don't let excuses or cowardice rob you of this crown.

3. *The crown of life.* "Happy is the man who doesn't give in and do wrong when he is tempted, for afterwards he will get as his reward the crown of life that God has promised those who love him" (James 1:12). This one is earned by endurance that is energized by love. You know that stamina is based on condition; if you're in good spiritual shape when temptation comes you'll win that battle now and gain the crown of life later.

4. *The crown of glory.* "Feed the flock of God; care for it willingly, not grudgingly; not for what you will get out of it, but because you are eager to serve the Lord. Don't be tyrants, but lead them by your good example, and when the Head Shepherd comes, your reward will be a never-ending share in his glory and honor" (1 Peter 5:2-4). Some pastors will win this one, but

each of us has a sphere of influence and we can serve the family of God in many ways. Our example to our fellow Christians is very important.

5. *The crown of righteousness.* "In heaven a crown is waiting for me which the Lord, the righteous Judge, will give me on that great day of his return. And not just to me, but to all those whose lives show that they are eagerly looking forward to his coming back again" (2 Timothy 4:8). The signs Jesus told us to watch for are happening all around us in this generation. The next chapter will help you prepare for winning this crown.

What to do today:

Memorize the names and ways to gain the crowns and concentrate on whichever one you feel least able to win.

HE'S COMING BACK!

"I can tell you this directly from the Lord: that we who are still living when the Lord returns will not rise to meet him ahead of those who are in their graves. For the Lord himself will come down from heaven with a mighty shout and with the soul-stirring cry of the archangel and the great trumpet-call of God. And the believers who are dead will be the first to rise to meet the Lord. Then we who are still alive and remain on the earth, will be caught up with them in the clouds to meet the Lord in the air and remain with him forever. So comfort and encourage each other with this news" (1 Thessalonians 4:15-18).

"When is all this going to happen? I really don't need to say anything about that, dear brothers, for you know perfectly well that no one knows. That day of the Lord will come unexpectedly like a thief in the night. When people are saying, 'All is well, everything is quiet and peaceful' — then, all of a sudden, disaster will fall upon them as suddenly as a woman's birth pains begin when her child is born. And these people will not be able to get away anywhere — there will be no place to hide" (5:1-3).

The enemies of God will not be ready for Jesus' return, but notice what Paul says to God's people. "But, dear brothers, you are not in the dark about these things, and you won't be surprised as by a thief when the day of the Lord comes. For you are all children of the light and of the day, and do not belong to the darkness and night. So be on your guard, not asleep like the others. Watch for his return. For God has not chosen to pour out his anger upon us, but to save us through our Lord Jesus Christ; he died for us so that we can live with him forever, whether we are dead or alive at the time of his return. So encourage each other to build each other up" (5:4-6, 9-11).

The mention of Christ's coming back for us occurs 380 times in the New Testament! Only four of the twenty-seven books omit reference to it. That averages out to one out of every twenty-five verses! It doesn't take a super-intellect to deduce that God is trying to get our attention about a very important event, so we do well to pay attention.

Jesus told of specific signs that would increase in frequency and intensity — these signs are happening *now!* Wars, earthquakes, lawlessness, astrology, Satan worship, heart-failure from fear, increase in knowledge and travel, Israel's nationhood, and other events described in Matthew 24 seem to be happening before our eyes. I recommend you read my book *Orbit of Ashes* for a detailed accounting of the events of the end times. (Tyndale House, $1.25)

The second coming of Christ is often referred to as "the blessed hope" after the phrase in Titus 2:13 (King James Version) and because it is the supreme anticipation of Christians. We need to encourage each other with this hope when evil men and forces seem to be destroying the good things of life. You and I might never change the goals of the White House or the United Nations, but God will use us to change individuals — who change society — and eventually we will be transported to the perfect society in heaven.

"Now we can look forward to the salvation God has promised us. There is no longer any room for doubt, and we can tell others that salvation is ours, for there is no question that he will do what he says. In response to all he has done for us, let us outdo each other in being helpful and kind to each other and in doing good. Let us not neglect our church meetings, as some people do, but encourage and warn each other, especially now that the day of his coming back again is drawing near" (Hebrews 10:23-25).

What to do today:

"Dear friends, while you are waiting for these things to happen and for him to come, try hard to live without sinning; and be at peace with everyone so that he will be pleased with you when he returns. And remember why he is waiting. He is giving us time to get his message of salvation out to others" (2 Peter 3:14, 15).

Here's something else to do. Get alone somewhere and read the following. (We started the month with joy because "the joy of the Lord is your strength," and we'll end it the same.)

"Now all praise to God for his wonderful kindness to us and his favor that he has poured out upon us, because we belong to his dearly loved Son. So overflowing is his kindness toward us that he took away all our sins through the blood of his Son, by whom we are saved; and he has showered down upon us the riches of his grace

— for how well he understands us and knows what is best for us at all times.

"God has told us his secret reason for sending Christ, a plan he decided on in mercy long ago; and this was his purpose: that when the time is ripe he will gather us all together from wherever we are — in heaven or on earth — to be with him in Christ, forever. Moreover, because of what Christ has done we have become gifts to God that he delights in. . . . God's purpose in this was that we should praise God and give glory to him for doing these mighty things for us, who were the first to trust in Christ.

"And because of what Christ did, all of you others too, who heard the Good News about how to be saved, and trusted Christ, were marked as belonging to Christ by the Holy Spirit, who long ago had been promised to all of us Christians. His presence within us is God's guarantee that he will really give us all that he promised; and the Spirit's seal upon us means that God has already purchased us and that he guarantees to bring us to himself. This is just one more reason for us to praise our glorious God" (Ephesians 1:6-14).

31

NOW WHAT?

You've made a good start. Keep going. Remember, these daily vitamins and exercises aren't just for a month — by continuing to use them you'll get stronger and more discerning. You'll sense the Holy Spirit's power within you and you'll know and do God's will.

I know God is pleased with you and the growth you've made. Determine to delight him more — and enrich your life — by continuing to grow in spirit and in truth.

"When I think of the wisdom and scope of his plan I fall down on my knees and pray to the Father of all the great family of God . . . that out of his glorious, unlimited resources he will give you the mighty inner strengthening of his Holy Spirit. And I pray that Christ will be more and more at home in your hearts, living within you as you trust in him. May your roots go down deep into the soil of God's marvelous love; and may you be able to feel and understand, as all God's children should, how long, how wide, how deep, and how high his love really is; and to experience this love for yourselves, though it is so great that you never see the end of it or fully know or understand it. And so at last you will be filled up with God himself" (Ephesians 3:14-19).